DON'T SMOTHER YOUR DRAGON

BUILDING A HEALTHY WRITING CAREER

J.S. DIXON

NANETTE M. DAY

Series   link-   https://www.amazon.com/J-S-Dixon/e/B07YGXWP1K/

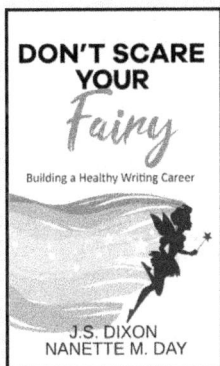

Don't Scare Your Fairy: Building a Healthy Writing Career

Keep your fairy happy and flappy!

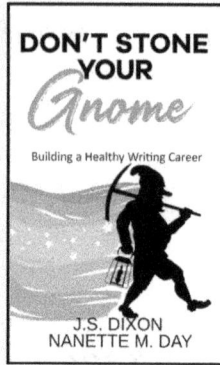

Don't Stone Your Gnome: Building a Healthy Writing Career

Protect your gnome—after all, it's your name on the line.

Series link- https://www.amazon.com/J-S-Dixon/e/B07YGXWP1K/

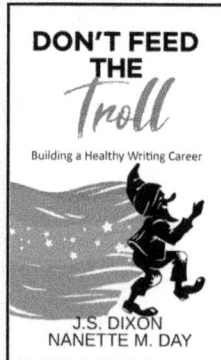

Don't Feed the Troll: Building a Healthy Writing Career

Keep those trolls where they belong: under the bridge!

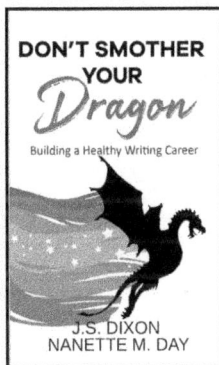

Don't Smother Your Dragon: Building a Healthy Writing Career

Your dragon will fly fast and fly confidently

FOREWORD

The Building a Healthy Writing Career series helps you succeed as a writer by nourishing your muse, heeding your inner voice, doing the work consistently, and eliminating time/energy drains from your workday. The individual books can be read in any order and include appendixes with additional resources.

INTRODUCTION

Welcome to *Don't Smother Your Dragon: Building a Healthy Writing Career*. We're glad to have you along for this wonderful journey into your writing career.

You're probably wondering how a dragon can help your writing process. Aren't dragons powerful and destructive beasts who eat humans for snacks? Sure, some dragons are quite the meanies, but our dragons —the beasts within us that give us the power and drive to succeed—are here to help us in our writing careers. We'll explain how to harness that power effectively in this book.

This book isn't fluff. If you want fluff, grab a teddy bear. This series is information for writers who want to be informed, stay informed, and get more done. It's a B.S.-free zone. We share the truth, and we keep it real, as the truth isn't always pretty.

We won't sugarcoat what you need to do and what can go wrong. We, Jules and Nanette, are happy people. Butterflies and rainbows shoot from our lips on a daily basis. Yeah, maybe not quite that happy. The normal amount of happy, plus a dash. We know that not everything's going to be butterflies and rainbows all the time, but we do our best to stay focused on the end goal: producing good writing consistently.

This book isn't gospel. We aren't preaching to you that this is the only way to succeed as a writer. Rather, we noticed that many writers in our support groups were facing the same challenges as we were, and we decided to share the methods, techniques, and insights that have worked for us to keep us on track.

You are the CEO of your writing career, but the reading population can make or break your authorship. And it is a ship. It's floating in rough and calm waters. It's vulnerable to distractions and misdirection. When you're lost at sea, you might experience all sorts of hallucinations that entice you to leave your charted path and head into really dangerous waters. We call this Shiny Object Syndrome (SOS). Whether it's the sirens luring you to your death or some newfangled gadget or service that promises to make you a best-selling author, these shiny objects can kill a writing career by forcing you to deviate from your path to success and hit that proverbial iceberg. By following a few simple tips and hints, you can ignore all those shiny objects (that promise the world but never deliver) and keep smoothly sailing to build the successful writing career you envision for yourself.

So that's what this book isn't. But there are a million things this book is. We won't bore you with 999,997 of them because you're going to find out, but the top three that we want you to know about are: experience, candid delivery, and take-it-or-leave-it advice.

Cumulatively, Jules and Nanette have two decades of writing experience, and we've written more than 60 published works of all sizes, from micro-fiction to 100K+-word novels in a variety of genres, from LGBT romance to sweet holiday stories to grit lit stories that would make even the most terrifying dragons cower and whimper.

We know how hard writing is and that the industry changes constantly. What we're giving you is our knowledge and what we've researched from other authors who have also been there and done that. We've faced everything you're probably going through. We love writing and we want to help you love it, love it again, or love it even more, depending on where you are in your writing life cycle.

This book contains candid delivery with a little humor. We play up the "dragon" angle to help you understand just how powerful your visions of success can be in driving your writing career forward. We also include Action Steps that will help you set a well-defined course to avoid all the shiny objects that might be distracting you from your career path. We want to help you approach your writing career with a focus on maximizing success while still embracing the creative freedom that first attracted you to writing. Jules isn't a fan of sugar coating anything except for the rim of her sweettart martini, and Nanette lives in the middle of the country where she makes cows cry, so we're going to be honest and persuasive. That's a promise.

Ultimately, this is your career. We understand that. You get to decide what you will and won't take from this. We can guide you, but the writer is the one who determines their success. If you decide to disregard the advice and information we provide, all we would ask is that you let us know what you did differently and how it worked. Writing can be a solitary endeavor, but we're here for you and we won't judge. We've developed a Facebook community and we welcome you to join us; even if you just lurk, you're welcome.

Okay, it's time. Are you ready to harness the power of the dragon to build an effective writing process and achieve all your dreams of success? Let's get to it!

1-FINDING YOUR SPARK

When we think about successful people, we often focus on how they succeeded despite tremendous hardships. You've likely heard about the life stories of J. K. Rowling, who was jobless and raising a young child alone when she wrote the Harry Potter books (which twelve publishing houses passed on before she sold her manuscripts), and Oprah Winfrey, who was physically and sexually abused as a child and fired from her first job for being unfit for television. Stephen King's first book, *Carrie*, was rejected by thirty publishers before being accepted, and Dr. Seuss failed his doctoral studies program, dropped out of school, and was rejected dozens of times before selling his first story. These people would not give up on their dreams, no matter what hurdles life threw up in their paths.

They ultimately succeeded because they let their inner fires burn brightly.

Call it determination, motivation, strength, drive ... whatever word you prefer, your inner fire gives you the power to move further along your path even when you feel like it is impossible to continue. In this book, we're going to talk about your dragon, which is how we refer to your inner fire and the passion that drives you to succeed. Sephora, a particularly powerful dragon with a red-hot inner fire, will be joining us to help figure out how to build your own inner fire, how to stoke the flames, and how to ensure that the fire doesn't consume you.

Before we can ignite and build our own inner fires, it is important to understand what your dragon is and what it isn't.

Our dragons come in all shapes and sizes, and they survive (and thrive) on different kinds of fuels, but there are some similarities that all dragons share. A dragon does not simply appear. It is discovered, chosen, created, and shaped. Your dragon should excite you and animate you; in doing so, it will empower you. Your dragon does not hide from or abandon you either, although if you don't take care of it, you run the risk of smothering the fire (which is not a good thing). A healthy, well-cared-for dragon burns from the inside out, not from the outside in. We're going to talk about all these ideas in the next chapter.

Action Step #1

Set a time and spend one minute brainstorming. List everything that excites you. Include activities, events, smells, tastes, sounds, feelings, and experiences in all areas of your life. Jot down everything that comes to mind.

When you're done, review your list. Do you notice any common threads? How can you incorporate items from this list into your daily life? (Bonus: Do any of the listed items fit your stories and/or characters for your current work in progress? Try injecting aspects of your excitement into your writing, when appropriate).

This is a great activity to do on a regular basis, like once a month or once a quarter. Compare your lists over time to see how the things that excite you are changing.

2-BUILDING YOUR INNER FIRE

Humans are born with an inherent will to live, which is why our body signals us when we need to eat, drink, and sleep. We are biologically hardwired to survive.

But surviving is much different than thriving, and if you're reading this book, it's because you want to thrive in your writing career. How you define "thrive" is unique to you, and we'll talk more about that later in this chapter, but for now realize that, biologically speaking, you are not necessarily built to thrive.

Sephora just huffed. She doesn't like that idea because she believes that humans are all built to thrive, but many of them don't realize it. Why wouldn't someone realize that they can (and should) thrive? The two most common reasons are that they are afraid to succeed or they fall victim to the procrastination demons.

A fear of success sounds like a foreign idea to many, but it's not as strange as you might think. The truth is that it is not the success itself we fear, but the results of the success. Imagine your latest novel or article suddenly goes viral for all the right reasons: it's a great story, told well, that readers connect with. People are talking about your writing, and they're asking you all sorts of questions. How did you come up with the idea? How did you feel while writing it? Did you ever expect it would resonate so strongly with readers around the world?

Many of you might be excited to think about such success, but others might become anxious. Those who feel the tingles of anxiety starting could be worried about our fellow writers, who will surely see through the blind luck of our success and recognize that we are just faking this whole writing career. Such fear plays into imposter syndrome, which we talked about in *Don't Feed the Troll*. Imposter syndrome makes you believe that you are a failure despite evidence to the contrary. Someone who suffers from imposter syndrome (which can strike when you least expect it) would experience an exacerbated form of it if they were to produce a bestseller because now the whole world can see just how big of a fake they are.

In addition, success could bring about more attention from various areas in our lives, including friends and family members, local communities, and social media. Unfortunately, not all such attention will be positive. We might worry that, instead of spending our days writing, we will be forced to defend ourselves in at least a few of those discussions. What if people start tweeting untruths about us as a writer? Should we react and, if so, how? What if a local newspaper does a story on our success and we lose control of the narrative? What if our neighbors start talking about us, commenting that now we must be making the kind of money that the Harry Potter series generated simply because we had a successful book or one of our articles was published in an international journal?

Again, some people would welcome such attention if it comes from successful writing, but others jump through all sorts of hoops to avoid even the possibility of such a scenario, even when it means sabotaging our own writing careers. You might fall somewhere along this spectrum, perhaps worrying that you're not as good of a writer as you think you are so any success would not be earned. Or maybe you think you are a good writer but a lack of success after you publish would somehow prove to you in your mind that you aren't really as good as you thought.

Such fears can be incredibly deep-seated within our brains, and we might be taking actions (or inactions) that impede our writing production without even realizing it. Nanette has become a master of all sorts of self-sabotage and avoidance in her writing career, so she's going to share some examples throughout this book, but even if all of this sounds completely foreign to you, we'll be sharing tips that will benefit you in building the fiercest and fieriest dragon you can so you continue to produce content.

But if you have even the slightest tinge of concern somewhere deep in your brain that any of these scenarios could become a reality, you might unknowingly sabotage your own efforts to succeed even before you write your first sentence. You might even engage in avoidance strategies that are actually training your brain that such fear is a good thing. How many times have you found yourself going down yet another rabbit hole while searching for the perfect character name so you can start writing your novel or looking for the ideal graphic to pair with an article you have yet to write? You might be able to convince yourself that you really are working, but ultimately how much writing do you actually get done? Zilch. Such avoidance strategies dovetail right into procrastination and, in the end, you are tossing a wet blanket on the embers of your inner fire, which won't make your dragon very happy.

Creating Your Dragon

Okay, before this book gets too depressing (Jules here: Too late), let's talk about how you can create your own dragon—how you can create the motivation and drive to produce new content day after day, even when you might want to chase that rabbit down its most meandering hole.

Notice that we said "create your own dragon." In *Don't Scare Your Fairy* we talked about creating a writing practice that attracted your muse to you, keeping her healthy so she stuck around. Fairies (muses) exist all around us. We have to search to find them, then keep them happy.

However, your dragon is a different kind of creature, because it is unique to you. It belongs to you alone. It does not exist until you create it. It does not simply appear in your life. You must do the work to discover which dragon suits your needs, create that dragon, choose the right approach to ensure that it stays alive with you, and shape it to change as your needs change.

Yes, it's a lot of work, and it's never-ending work. But creating a dragon that roars to life when you need it (whether you realize you need it or not) is one of the strongest tools you can cultivate in your healthy writing career. Your dragon will not hide or abandon you, although if you don't take care of it or let your fears take over, you run the risk of smothering your dragon's fire (which defeats the whole purpose of creating your dragon to begin with).

The overarching question to ask when creating your dragon seems so simple: What drives you? Unfortunately, many people cannot answer this question or they don't answer it deeply enough. We're going to take a few minutes here to really delve into this question so you can start the process for creating your dragon.

You might want to grab a pen and paper or open a new file on your computer so you can jot down ideas as they come to you. Take as much time as you need thinking about your answers, your situation, and your personal goals; review and revise them over the next few days and weeks, as necessary. The more comprehensive you can be, the healthier your baby dragon will be. (We'll talk about ways to nurture your new dragon in the "Stoking Your Inner Fire" chapter.)

Okay, back to that question: What drives you?

Let's start with an example response: being a successful writer. This answers the question, but it is not a motivator that will enable you to create your dragon because it doesn't delve deeply enough into your goals. For example, how do you define success? Is it completing and publishing three novels? Okay, let's say you write and publish five novels, but no one buys them—well, not enough people buy them to cover your expenses (e.g., covers, editing). Are you successful?

Some people might be happy to simply enjoy the experience of writing, but if you're reading this book because you want to build a healthy writing career, you probably want to do more than simply write and publish.

So what does success mean to you? Is it money? If so, how much? Enough to quit your job and write full time? Enough to take your dream vacation? Enough to buy a house or pay off your mortgage? Enough to cover your kids' college tuition? Enough for you to retire?

Maybe you define success by the number of fans or followers you have. Is that the number of dedicated fans in your street team? The number of social media followers? The number of people who sign up (and read) your newsletter? The number of people who attend a reading? How many is enough for you to consider yourself successful?

Perhaps you define success by being recognized by your colleagues. What does this look like? Is it being invited to speak at national and international conferences? Being asked to teach classes on writing? Being asked to guest write articles and blog posts on some aspect of writing? Having your book, stories, or articles included in the curriculum for a prestigious writing or literature course?

Maybe you define success as a combination of several factors. Perhaps you'd like to be able to quit your non-writing job so you can write full time, have enough money to cover health insurance and build a small nest egg, have at least five thousand newsletter subscribers who open and read your newsletter every time you send it out, and be asked to teach a writing class at the local college.

Okay, so you now have a general idea about what your success will look like, but we're not finished defining what drives you. Sticking with the "successful writer" response, it is also important to consider time frames you expect for your success. When do you want to be this "successful writer"? We're not looking at a "do or die" deadline here. We're simply talking about when you envision your success, when it is happening? If it is happening further out in the future, like a decade or more, it might be harder for you to feel motivated today—it's possible, but you might have to do a little more work in nurturing your dragon and keeping its fires stoked.

We're also not talking about an "all-or-nothing" deadline. Maybe you want to start seeing some aspects of success by the time all your kids are attending school full time. Perhaps you want to see enough monetary success that you can quit your non-writing job as soon as you get certain bills paid off. Maybe you want to focus on building your newsletter subscribers and reaching a certain number before your next publication.

Hopefully you're realizing that defining what drives you is a fluid and multifaceted process that has varying timelines. But no matter what you focus on when determining what drives you, you must remember that your dragon should excite you and animate you. If it does, it will empower you to build new, greater visions of success. If it doesn't, it will leech your fire from you until you become an ashy remnant of your former self.

Shaping an Exciting Dragon

As you are defining what motivates you in order to create your own dragon, you will likely come up with all sorts of ideas. Some are tried and true. Some might seem wild and "out there." As you start down this path of discovery, nothing should be discarded. Take note of every idea that comes to mind. Later, you can explore them in more depth to determine if they are valid drivers for you.

Some of your ideas might actually be flukes that go nowhere. For example, you might decide that what drives you is writing murder mysteries. You develop your plan, nurture your dragon, stoke the fires, and delve into your first series. However, somewhere along the way, you discover that it is not the stories themselves that excite you, but rather the research on real-life murder mysteries.

At this point, you might need to sit down and have a serious heart-to-heart talk with your dragon because, instead of writing mysteries, you decide to develop a podcast discussing true crime. That's okay! Your dragon will be much more powerful and better able to keep that fire inside you burning brightly if you are honest with it (and yourself).

Shaping your dragon is an important process to master because what drives you to keep pushing forward, even when you don't want to, will change over time. It is inevitable. Think about where you were five years ago or ten years ago. Five (ish) years ago, Jules was finishing her first series and was preparing to publish it independently. She had a goal of writing two novels a year, publishing them, and building her fan base. Today she is publishing 25 books every three months, is a hybrid author (both independently publishing and working with a publisher), has expanded into non-fiction books and articles on sites like Medium, has served as an editor and publisher of multiple anthologies, and is making presentations at various conferences (something she never planned to do). All of these achievements were the direct result of her evolving definition of success and her efforts to shape her dragon as a result.

Even if you don't believe that what drives you will change and evolve over time, remember that as writers we rely on others to produce our stories and articles, whether that be magazines and blogs or platforms like Amazon and Barnes & Noble—and they are all changing every day. The publishing industry has changed dramatically over the last decade, in the process redefining how writers can share their work.

So you might not change, but the world around you will, and those changes will affect how you define what makes your dragon the fiercest creature possible.

You might also realize that some aspects of your definition of success do not move you forward as you expected. For example, perhaps you decide to participate in three book signings a year as a way to connect with your readers. However, no matter what you do to ensure a respectable turnout, the signings attract the same handful of readers looking for freebies each time. In this case, you might decide that this component of your success definition is no longer worth pursuing, so you drop it and move on.

Ultimately, shaping your dragon is an ongoing process. Take a few weeks to really drill down and define what you want to achieve in your writing career, but after you use that information to shape your dragon, you will need to periodically revisit how you shaped your dragon to make sure it still fits your goals and needs.

We suggest building time into your schedule to revisit what motivates you and how you have built your dragon based on those motivators. Some people might do this once a year. New Year's is a popular time to reflect on your current situation and decide what is working, what is not, and what you want to work on next. However, remember that people often get caught up in the holiday season and envision quite lofty goals around this time of year.

If you find yourself falling into the New Year's trap (and it is a trap because when you can't meet those unrealistic goals you might beat yourself up, which will make your dragon extinguish its fire in a heartbeat), try setting up quarterly meetings with your dragon to talk about where you are and where you want to be. Set up appointments in your electronic calendar so you are reminded of it, then go to a place that feels rejuvenating and positive for you (e.g., a favorite restaurant, a local park, an art museum) and work through the entire "What drives you?" process once again. Create a vision and define your stepping-stones along the path to that vision.

Fuel your dragon with the information it needs to keep your fire burning brightly.

Caring for Your Dragon

A healthy, well-cared-for dragon burns from the inside out, not from the outside in. The information you feed your dragon comes from you: your visions, your expectations, your hopes, your dreams. It is an incredibly personal experience that is unique to you and your dragon, and you cannot replicate what someone else does and expect to have the same outcome.

In fact, when creating, shaping, and nurturing your dragon, you should listen to only one voice: yours. If you incorporate external expectations, it will extinguish your dragon's fire.

People often turn to others to help define their own drive and goals. This happens all the time and in ways we might not be aware of. Just think about the last time you told someone you were a writer. What was their reaction? Perhaps they asked what kinds of books you write. Such a reaction already sets up an expectation for you that you will not meet if you are writing for journals or online magazines. You might have just published your third article in *The New Yorker*, but that success will not meet the expectations of this other person, which can leave you feeling deflated in your success.

Or maybe you did just publish a book, but when you tell the curious other person that it was a romance novel, they arch an eyebrow and comment, "Oh, cashing in on that whole *Fifty Shades* craze, eh?" You might offer them a quick overview on the difference types of romance—sweet romance, clean romance, hot and steamy romance, erotic romance—and where erotica does and doesn't fit, but again the excitement you had a minute ago about publishing a new novel is dampened now, and the fires of your dragon are burning a little less brightly.

Fitting others' expectations is actually the path of

least resistance when it comes to defining what drives you. It sounds counterintuitive, but think about it a moment: Others' expectations are based on predefined and accepted roles in society. You've likely seen those memes on social media that include a series of six photos depicting different aspects of a writer's life: what my friends think I do, what my parents think I do, what society thinks I do, what my publisher thinks I do, what I think I do, what I really do. All of them have a kernel of truth to them, but you cannot use those truths to motivate you to write or, sad to say, you won't get much writing done.

A successful writer writes. Period.

But friends, family, and society expect a successful writer to publish. There's a big difference between writing and publishing, and if publishing is not in your personal definition of success, then even when you are writing (and, thus, succeeding) the people around you will be signaling to you that you are not actually successful.

Don't accept predefined roles and visions of success because they will not fit your unique situation. You must define what you want for yourself. It takes more work, but the payoffs in the long run are so much better. Plus, when you run into someone who tries to suggest that you are not being as driven or successful as you should be, you will feel more confident in your achievements (whether recognized or not).

Don't worry. Your dragon's got your back.

Action Step #2

What drives you? Envision your future life when you have achieved the success you desire. What is your typical day like in this future successful life? What do you spend your time doing during the week? On the weekends? Where do you live: in the city, country, forest, mountains, beach? In a house, apartment, cabin, motorhome? With whom? How is your home decorated? What does it smell like?

What kinds of clothes do you wear? How do they feel against your skin? What kind of transportation do you use (e.g., kind of car you drive)? What do you eat and drink? What do you see from your workspace window? What is the weather like? Do you have kids? Pets? Chickens?

What do you do during your free time? What sports and/or hobbies do you participate in? What is your favorite place to visit and how often do you go? What special events do you participate in (both career related and family/personal related)? Where do you vacation? What are your holidays like?

Take a few moments to describe your successful life, including sights, sounds, smells, tastes, and feelings. Write your vision down or record it as a voice file or video recording. Revisit this exercise at least once a year to see how your vision has changed.

Whenever you might be feeling less than motivated to get your work done, pull out your vision and read/listen/watch it. During your scheduled breaks, look for pictures that fit your vision (e.g., of your future home or location). Hang those pictures in your workspace or some other area where you will see them every day. Take a few moments every day to look at the pictures you have collected and remind yourself that you are moving along the path to get to your dream life.

3-NURTURING YOUR DRAGON

Having a vision of where you want your writing career to go is a critical step in the healthy and successful writing career. When we think about people who succeeded despite the challenges they faced, we know that success did not simply fall in their laps. Successful people have a vision for their future and they take definitive steps to move along the path that leads to that future.

Nurturing your inner fire is important for a variety of reasons, which we discuss in this chapter.

Improving Your Efficiency

When you have a clear vision of where you want to go, you can make your journey to the destination more efficient. One of the most important results of a clear vision is that you are able to clarify your short- and long-term goals, both of which are necessary to ensure that you succeed.

Think about the vision you developed in the previous chapter. Some parts of the vision might require longer-term goals. For example, maybe you want to live in a cabin in the woods, isolated from the world, spending your mornings writing articles about the natural world while the afternoons are reserved for hiking. A long-term goal would be gathering the funds necessary to purchase the cabin and land. A short-term goal might be developing a morning writing routine. You can start working on that short-term goal right away and enjoy the fruits of your success, which will move you further along the path to your ultimate vision of success.

You can also streamline and prioritize your work tasks. If you know you want to focus on writing about the natural world, such as woodland creatures, the environment, and off-the-grid living, you can start building your audience in these areas. Your end goal might be to write a series of books, but while working out the organization of the books you can start honing your skills by writing articles for online platforms and print magazines. You can subsequently use these articles as the building blocks for your future books.

Knowing where you want to go makes the trip easier. Imagine you are in Atlanta and you want to visit a friend who lives in New York City—Queens, to be exact. You get into your car, knowing you have to head north, but without knowing your friend's address. Sure, you can probably find your way to the interstate easily enough, and you make great time traveling toward your destination at first.

But once you get to New York City, you are not sure where to go. You don't have a map or GPS, so you decide to just drive until you find your destination. You might stop and ask people if they know your friend and where she lives. Most people have never heard of your friend. Some people give you bad directions, sending you off into the wilds of New Jersey. Others try to convince you to abandon your journey and come out to party with them.

Needless to say, if you ever do find your friend's house (and that's a big if), it is days and even months after you started your journey. You have wasted time and money (gas isn't cheap) driving to places far off your path. In fact, it takes you so long to find your friend's house that by the time you arrive, she no longer lives there!

If you wouldn't be so lackadaisical when visiting a friend, why would you be that way when making decisions about your writing career?

When we get caught up in tasks that do not move us forward or spend all our energy on activities that do not stoke our inner fire, we are more likely to become demotivated because it feels like we're spinning our wheels and not getting anywhere.

Building a writing career is hard work. Don't waste your energy on tasks that don't lead you further along the path to your ultimate vision of success. Use your vision of success to clarify your short- and long-term goals, set priorities, and focus on tasks that move you forward.

Making You Stronger

Having a vision of where you want your writing career to go and nurturing your dragon also makes you stronger as an individual. (Please note: Do not use your dragon to strongarm others. Leave that to George R. R. Martin.)

When you have a vision of your ultimate success, it creates a sense of stability in your writing work. You know where you will end up. You know the steps you need to take to get there. Now you must simply follow the road signs.

On our imaginary trip to Queens without using a map or GPS, we would quickly start questioning our decision, which is a huge fire extinguisher for any dragon. When we question ourselves in such situations, we are sowing the seeds of self-doubt, which can quickly bloom as imposter syndrome.

Self-doubt can be toxic to a writing career. It can

start as simply as questioning whether a description is appropriate, but then morph into questions about whether we should even be writing at all. When we are gripped by self-doubt, we can become paralyzed in our writing, unable to complete a story or a paragraph or even a sentence. We might not even be able to start to write in the first place.

However, knowing where we are going and how we are getting there gives us stability in our writing, even when experiencing episodes of self-doubt. When we find ourselves suddenly questioning whether we will ever finish our current work in progress, we can look at our vision once again and remind ourselves that we have already travelled partway down the path. Rather than allowing our doubt to lead us down a rabbit hole and avoid writing, we remember that writing through the doubt will get us to the other side. Sure, we will have to edit what we are writing at this point with a somewhat stronger red pen, but we are still getting the words on the page and moving one step closer to our vision of success.

In addition, each time we persevere in such situations, we are retraining our brains. Whereas before we might have avoided writing because of a fear of success or a wave of procrastination, now our brain is learning that we can (and must!) write despite these challenges that keep popping up. Because let's face it: Challenges will always show up when we are trying to press forward. The challenges may be external or internal. By nurturing our dragon and fanning the flames of our inner fire, we are teaching our brain that the answer to overcoming any and all problems is simple: write.

As we continue to write due to our stability and ability to persevere in challenging situations, we are also building our self-confidence, which is the best way to ward off imposter syndrome. Each time we overcome a challenge, we become more confident in our abilities and in the idea that we deserve the success we are aiming for. This self-confidence is not based on some idea that we are the best writer ever, but rather that when we put our butt in the chair and start typing or writing, words will come, sentences will emerge, and stories will evolve.

Remember, a successful writer is someone who writes. Each time you write, you are nurturing your dragon, strengthening your fire, and reaffirming that you are a successful writer. Just stay the course and you will achieve what you set out to accomplish.

Attracting a Community

Nurturing your dragon also attracts others to you. When you are a successful writer, meaning you write, others see that and want to emulate you. Other writers want to be like you, and they will be curious about how you achieve your success.

More importantly (perhaps—depending on how you define success), readers will be attracted to you. Readers like to build relationships with writers in that they look for the next story the writer writes. As a writer who is nurturing your dragon to follow your plan to achieving success, you are producing more and more content, which gives readers more chances to connect with you. Each connection strengthens that relationship, turning readers into fans and even super-fans. You can learn more about building meaningful relationships with readers in *Don't Stone Your Gnome.*

As you progress along your path to success, others will join you, cheering you on and supporting you in your endeavors, which can generate a sense of satisfaction that motivates you even more.

Creating Satisfaction

When you are following your path to success, staying on task, achieving short- and long-term goals, building a stable writing process, becoming more self-confident, and attracting supporters, you are creating a stronger sense of satisfaction, which is the healthiest drug in the world for your inner fire. Seriously, the feeling of satisfaction is like throwing gasoline on your inner fire. (Sephora just chuckled. She really likes the satisfaction drug.)

What's even better is that when you are satisfied

with your work, you tend to become even more productive. In other words, staying true to your vision will likely lead you to even greater success than you expected. If a successful writer writes, then a satisfied successful writer writes even more!

Defining your vision is important for creating a plan for success, but you must also nurture your dragon to ensure that you don't get lost along the way. The more you can nurture your dragon, the stronger your inner fire becomes and the more productive you become. It's a cycle of empowering productivity that we can continue to build on throughout our writing careers, as long as we remember to check in with our vision of success and update it as necessary to ensure that it is always a place we want to make our own.

Action Step #3

Let's look at your vision of success again. We're going to use the cabin in the woods vision (writing in the mornings, hiking in the afternoons) as an example for this Action Step. Pick one area to focus on and identify the stepping-stones that will lead you to that part of your vision. Think about everything that needs to change or could be affected for you to achieve that part of the vision. This is a brainstorming activity, so don't discard any possibility.

For example, we want to focus on building a

morning writing routine. Currently we work a nine-to-five job. Possible options for writing in the morning include getting up earlier so we can write for an hour or two before we go to work, changing our schedule at work, finding a new job, working part time, and quitting our job altogether so we can focus on writing.

Now look at each of those options and consider the pros and cons as well as what accommodations you will need to make if you choose that path. For example, if we get up earlier to write before going to work, we will need to go to bed earlier. We might want to shift some of our other activities around; instead of going to the gym before work, now we go over our lunch break. But going to the gym helped get our creative juices flowing, so now if we're going to write in the morning, we need to incorporate some sort of workout to help us wake up. Perhaps fifteen minutes of yoga or running the dog around the neighborhood? Of course, we don't want to have to wake up too early, and we know our writing time will be strictly limited because we are fitting it in before going to a job. We realize that if, before going to bed the night before, we spend an hour organizing our writing space, jotting down notes, perhaps outlining the scene we want to write the next morning, then when we sit down to write, we don't have to spend our precious limited time thinking about what we want to do. In addition, we don't want to spend our morning hours making breakfast when we could be writing, so we add instant cereals and yogurt to our shopping list (i.e., grab-and-go options) —as well as really strong coffee to help us wake up.

Repeat this process for each of the possible options you identified, no matter how farfetched they may seem. Rearranging work hours or quitting a job now to write full time might seem unrealistic, but when you start to define what needs to happen to get you to that point, you might discover that it's closer than you think or that there are alternative opportunities that can provide a bridge to that outcome.

As you can see, making a conscious decision to shift our priorities can have far-reaching effects in all areas of our lives. This activity is to help you start thinking about the shift and seeing where the changes need to be made so you can start building out (and achieving) actionable goals, which we will discuss in the next chapter.

4-STOKING YOUR INNER FIRE

Sephora is curled up in front of the fireplace, content with the fact that you are creating your own personal dragon to keep you on your path to success. She's pretending to be napping, enjoying the warmth of the fire, but really she is watching you, waiting to see what you do next.

She's such a smart dragon.

You see, even when you define what drives you to achieve, what gets the fires deep inside you burning so brightly that you have no choice but to continue working on your ultimate goal, it doesn't mean that you can sit back and relax. You have to continually stoke the fires of motivation or they will turn to ash and your dragon will cease to exist.

The extinction of dragons is a topic about which Sephora is incredibly passionate, as you can imagine, so we want to make sure that no dragons are lost because we forgot to fan the flames.

There are two ways to fan the flames and stoke the fire of your dragon: internally and externally. Internal efforts produce the best outcomes, so focus on those first. External efforts are important as well, but if you do the external efforts without doing the internal ones, your flames will at most be smoldering embers without ever really reaching the burning hot temperature necessary to drive you forward.

Internal Fanning of the Flames

Internal efforts that focus on stoking the fire of your dragon can be summed up as follows: Expect success. Prepare for success. Plan for success.

Expect Success

Expect success refers to visualizing success and being optimistic about your achievements. We've already done some visualizing practice in "Building Your Inner Fire" and Action Step #2, but you can use visualization in all aspects of your writing career. For example, each night as you lie in bed, before you drift off to sleep, visualize what the next day will be like for you. Picture yourself writing and experiencing satisfaction with your writing. Remember that, when you visualize, you should include as many details, including all five senses, as possible because that makes the vision more realistic, which makes it harder for your brain to derail your efforts.

Visualization is a powerful tool in your healthy writing career toolbox, but it is one that is often over-looked. Let's start with something simple. When you were first learning to walk as a baby, you might have been confused by stairs—and yes, even today stairs might be a challenge (Nanette raises her hand in agreement). How did you learn to walk up the stairs? A lot of it had to do with training your muscles, but how did you know you were supposed to walk up the stairs in the first place? Because you saw others doing it.

When we observe something happening, our brains create pathways along the nervous system. These pathways tell us that what we observed is one way to do something. Are you someone who learns by watching others do something? It's clear by all of the video tutorials on YouTube and elsewhere that this is a very common way of learning, and that is because it is a powerful way of learning.

Now, here's the beauty of the brain: It interprets mental images in the same way, so it doesn't matter whether you actually see something happening or you imagine it happening. Either way, your brain will accept it as reality and start building those pathways.

The stronger those pathways become, the more our brains tell our bodies to follow them.

Even if you've never actually done the action that you are visualizing, your brain tells your nervous system that you have. You are creating the expectation of success within the physical components of your body. The more practiced you become at visualization, the stronger your brain and nervous system will react.

Visualization should be as detailed as possible. This includes relying on all five senses, but also include your physical and emotional reactions to what you are visualizing. For example, if you are visualizing yourself standing in the doorway of your home, drinking your morning coffee, you might imagine what the sun feels like on your face. Do you turn your face toward it? Close your eyes? Enjoy the warmth? Maybe you are holding your coffee mug in both hands, letting the smell of fresh-brewed coffee waft over you as the mug warms your hands. You inhale deeply. What do feel when you do? A sense of content? Coziness? A surge of energy empowering you to conquer the day?

Visualization is best done without distractions, which is why we encourage you to incorporate a visualization practice at night, before you fall asleep, or in the mornings just after you wake up but before you get out of bed. You can also incorporate visual cues into your workday to remind you of your visualization. For example, if you picture yourself working in a specific location, have a picture of that location at hand so you can glance at it and instantly be reminded of your visualized success.

As powerful as visualization is as a tool, it is just that: a tool. If all you do is visualize, you will not succeed in achieving your goals. You'll just be wasting your time daydreaming. In order for visualization to be effective, you must act on the pathways that your brain is creating. Visualize yourself sitting at your desk and writing two thousand words, then go actually sit at your desk, turn on your computer, and start typing.

Another tool that you can use to build the expectation of success is optimism. (Jules just did a mental cartwheel.) (Jules here: And Nanette laughed at my attempt at gymnastics.) Optimism does not come naturally for all people and is a practiced trait, much like visualization. In fact, it can be combined with visualization to create a super powerful tool.

Optimism does not simply mean being hopeful. A key component of optimism is being confident and realistic in your optimism. Think of it this way: If you declare that you will write fifty full-length novels in the next six months, even if you say it in the most optimistic tone possible, it is not a realistic declaration for most people. What you have done is create a false optimism, and your brain isn't fooled. Neither is your dragon. The result is a zap to your self-confidence. Do this too many times and your attempts to be optimistic will actually erode your self-confidence.

Optimism helps you focus on your envisioned future goals. When you expect positive outcomes, you are more likely to make the choices that will lead you to that outcome. Visualizing your success while adopting an optimistic mindset will help you move beyond simply wanting something to actually going out and getting it.

Being optimistic and positive in your thinking involves several factors. You should speak in defined ways. For example, say "when I finish this project" (not if I finish...) or "I will complete this project by June." Note that, in English, the future verb construction of *will* + verb is more definitive than *going to* + verb. If you say "I am going to write three hundred words before lunch," you are telling your brain that you are planning to write. Whether you actually do write and achieve your goal is not the focus; the plan is. However, when you say "I will write three hundred words before lunch," you are telling your brain that the goal will be accomplished—no ifs, ands, or buts. It's a subtle difference that we may not even be aware of. Just make sure to use "will" instead of "going to." (Nanette is putting away her grammar geek hat now. Promise. [Now Jules is the one laughing.])

Optimism refers to both what you say out loud and your inner thoughts, and it's the latter area where many people struggle the most. If you find that inner voice being less than confidently optimistic, try writing down your thoughts periodically throughout the day. When you see them on paper, it can be easier to identify just where the optimism is weakening. Challenge any negative thoughts you might have. Make them positive. For example, while working on this chapter, Nanette was under deadline and constantly worrying (i.e., telling herself) that she was never going to get all the words written by said deadline, at which point Jules would ride her dragon over to Nanette and smite her. (Again, please no smiting. Dragons are not toys.) Once Nanette realized she was doing this, she shifted the focus from what she couldn't do to what she could. She would write five thousand words before dinner. As soon as she did that, the words started flowing. (By the way, she just hit six thousand words for the day and it is still an hour before dinner time.)

Being optimistic means speaking and thinking positively and in defined ways from a place of confidence. Challenge your negative thoughts. Create affirmations or mantras that you can repeat to yourself throughout the day. Use optimism to reinforce and strengthen the visualization you have created for yourself. And, just like visualizations, practice, practice, practice with optimism.

Using visualization and optimism together creates a powerful expectation of success within your brain and your entire body. That expectation strengthens your dragon and makes the motivational fires burn ever brighter.

Prepare for Success

When we prepare for success, we are stabilizing the pathway for our achievements. Think of it as creating a roadway to our checkpoints for success. At first, we might have a dirt road: functional, but not great during inclement weather, especially if there are still knots of roots from trees that have been cut down to make the path. (Nanette here: Also not great on the tush when you hit all those uneven bumps.) As we continue to use our road to visit our success checkpoints, we might get better at clearing away the stumps and roots and could even put gravel down, making it safer to navigate the roadway. The more we use it, the better we become at avoiding obstacles (like the raccoon family crossing the road) and the more permanent the road becomes until it's a paved highway connecting our efforts to success at rocket speeds.

It all sounds so easy, but preparing for success does not happen overnight. It is a process of identifying possible roadblocks and circumventing them or, even better, dismantling them before they slow us down. This process needs to happen outside of our dedicated writing time; if it doesn't, then we can get sidetracked, derailed, or sent down one of those pesky rabbit holes. In other words, we have to be aware of our surroundings, our processes, our habits, and our warning signs.

Preparing for success relies on two tools in our toolbox: journaling and meditating. Don't worry. We're not going to suggest that you spend excessive time on either of these tasks. In fact, as you become more adept at integrating them into your writing process, they should only require a few minutes every day.

We'll start with journaling. As writers, you may already engage in some form of journaling, whether it be stream of consciousness writing to clear out the cobwebs before focusing on your current project or brainstorming ideas for plot lines, articles, or future projects. All of that is wonderful, and we don't want you to stop doing any of that because journaling in its various forms can be really helpful in so many ways.

When you are focused on your vision of success, your journaling should enhance your efforts. You can do this by taking a minute or two before you start writing for the day to jot down some notes about your environment and your mood. Where are you working? What's the temperature like? What noises do you hear? Do you smell anything? How do you feel? What is your mindset when you start: determined to whip those words into shape, just trying to get over this bridge and on to greener pastures, or really not feeling it but determined to get words on the page? This is also a good time to practice your optimism by noting what you will accomplish in this writing session (remember to use "I will...").

When you are done with your writing session, repeat this journaling process, but this time focus on what you achieved during your session and how you feel about that achievement. You can note whether you accomplished the optimistic goal you set for yourself at the beginning, but also make sure that you identify other achievements as well. Perhaps you wrote a sentence that you are particularly proud of, or maybe you got a brilliant idea for a spin-off of your current project. Maybe you lost track of time while you were writing or finished an especially challenging passage.

When you identify these successes, also jot down a phrase or two about how each one made you feel. Connecting our emotions to our achievements is one way to strengthen the pathways that we create through our visualization practice. The stronger those pathways come, the more permanent they are and the easier it is for us to access them all the time.

As you get into the habit of this mini-journaling process, you can expand on it to include what you want to work on during your next writing session. Writing a sentence or two while you are ending one session is a great way to put you right back in the same mindset when you start your next session. It also helps remind you of all those positive feelings you experienced, which the brain will want to replicate.

Of course, sometimes you won't be jotting down all the positive successes that you achieved. Perhaps you feel frustrated at the end of your session because it took longer than expected or you kept getting interrupted because the dog wanted to go outside over and over and over. Make sure you note these things down too. Remember that this type of journaling is a component of the preparing for success, and you can't eliminate roadblocks if you don't see them. (Please don't eliminate the dog. He is not a roadblock.)

As you keep doing this journaling process, you should start to see patterns of what works best for you and what slows or impedes your writing. When you find something that works for you, pull out all the stops and make sure you use that discovery every time you can. Meanwhile, when you uncover a hurdle or roadblock, analyze the best way to deal with it. Should you go around it, bulldoze over it, or even build a new road? There's a bit of trial and error in this process, but by keeping notes on what is working and what isn't, it will be easier to identify real trends in your writing success instead of confusing them for caffeine-fueled word explosions.

The second part of the preparing for success is meditating. No you don't have to get your yoga mats out for this (although yoga is a great way to stretch out the muscles, especially after a writing marathon when you have been sitting at the computer for hours on end). You can meditate while sitting at your desk or in your favorite coffee shop. The one place we don't recommend meditating is while you are driving.

Meditating is a good way to start your writing session, doing it either before or after the journaling. It can also be beneficial when you need to take a break and re-center your focus. Some people might enjoy meditating at the end of their writing session as a way to reaffirm to their dragon that they enjoyed today's session and will return for more tomorrow. Whenever you meditate, try to do it at the same time, as this helps establish a ritual in your writing process, and rituals are great ways for eliminating distractions and focusing on the writing itself.

When you meditate, make sure you are in a comfortable position. Take several cleansing breaths and relax your muscles (think of them sinking into the chair or floor). You can meditate in silence or you might prefer to listen to gentle instrumental music, especially if you are meditating in a public place and need to block out noisy distractions. Close your eyes and open your mind. Let the thoughts flow in and out, without judging or even acknowledging them. All thoughts are welcome. If you have been stuck on a specific issue, you can use a question as a mantra, such as "Why is my heroine so afraid of her sibling?" Repeat this over and over while the thoughts flow in and out of your consciousness.

The idea behind meditation is that you are giving your brain a chance to process all the stimuli it is constantly experiencing without having to also work for you at the same time. Your mind is allowed to do whatever it wants for a change, and it uses this freedom to process information, make connections between that information, and generate new creative content. Meditation can clear out the clutter and make room for new discoveries. It creates a sense of calm and grounds us in a way that makes us more confident about the writing process as a whole.

Whether you meditate for five minutes or thirty minutes (or any length in between), make it a regular part of your writing process. Your mind will thank you, your inner voice will ooze confidence, and your dragon will burn with a fierce determination to succeed in achieving your writing goals.

Now that you have implemented your preparations for success, let's explore how you can plan for success.

Plan for Success

You might be thinking that so far everything we've been talking about is part of a plan for success. We're visualizing where we want to go, we're following our map and clearing barricades as we go, we're practicing optimism and reflecting on our successes and challenges while also giving our minds the freedom to be even more creative ... and *now* we're going to plan?

The short answer is yes.

Thus far we've been building an environment, both physical and mental, that will enable us to succeed in our writing careers. We've defined what success means to us, trained our brains what that success looks like, shifted our thinking to focus on achieving that success, and smoothed out the path to that success, but we haven't actually developed a plan to succeed yet. All of the tools we've discussed so far are beneficial in their own right, but without a plan, you are likely just spinning wheels.

When you plan for success, you are identifying specific, measurable, attainable, relevant, and time-bound goals. These are known as SMART goals. Everything we have been doing up to this point has given us the insights and information we need in order to create these goals for today, tomorrow, and far into the future.

A specific goal focuses on one target area. Saying "I want to become a successful writer" is not specific. As we discussed earlier, successful can mean different things to different people. When you define your goal, specificity is key. So you might say "I want to write a book." That's a little more specific, but we can go even deeper. Perhaps you want to write and publish a book.

And what will the book be about or what genre will it be? Will you independently publish or work with an established publisher? Taking all these areas into consideration, maybe you decide that your goal is as follows: I will write and independently publish a romantic comedy novel.

Okay, we've got the specificity down. Our next step is to determine how to measure our goal. In the previous example, the measurement is a novel—not a short story or a series. If you are writing articles, you might decide to measure the number of articles: I will write a three-article series about life as a single mom in rural America for publication on my blog.

The next step is to consider the attainability of the goal. Is your goal achievable? Does it align with your vision of success? Sure, you can argue that pretty much anything is achievable, but when you are building your goals, you want to make sure that they are something you can attain. If you want to write and publish a novel by the end of the month, but you work a full-time job, raise three kids, and spend your weekends taking care of a sick relative, you are going to be pretty hard pressed to find the fifteen hours a week that you need to write a sixty-thousand-word novel in a month. We're not saying you can't do it, but we want you to be able to enjoy the process, not feel pressured to accomplish a difficult goal. So as you are thinking about your goals, be realistic with what you can accomplish. Goals are meant to guide you to the finish line, not demotivate you so much that you quit the race halfway through.

We also need to make sure that our goals are relevant to our writing careers and to the vision of success we have created for ourselves. Achieving a goal of participating in three writing contests per year might be appropriate for some writers who are looking to challenge themselves and stretch their writing muscles, but if your vision of success is to pay off your mortgage, then participating in writing contests that require a fee or don't award cash prizes might not be the best goal for you at this time. The relevancy factor is important because you might set an easy goal because it is achievable. Great! You achieved it! So you do it again and again, each time enjoying the sense of accomplishment. But at the end of the year, you are no closer to achieving your vision of success because those goals—although achievable—were not relevant to your long-term career.

Finally, every goal should incorporate a time component. Going back to one of our previous examples, you might set the following goal: I will write and independently publish a romantic comedy novel within the next twelve months. We know this goal is specific and measurable. It is also achievable for you as you need to write at least five thousand words a month and you have set aside three hours a week for your writing. It is relevant to your vision of success as you want to produce a series of romantic comedy novels that you can also turn into screenplays. And it is time-bound as you have twelve months to complete the goal.

Once you have defined your goals, you can identify the objectives (i.e., tasks) you need to complete in order to achieve your goals (this is where the activity from Action Step #3 comes in handy). In the rom-com example, you know you need to write five thousand words a month, or just over a thousand words a week. As you will be independently publishing, you also need to build up your online presence, start a newsletter, find a cover designer and editor, and research the market. You can then break down your three hours of week into tasks that enable you to reach each milestone until you achieve the final goal.

Setting goals can be addictive, especially as you are able to enjoy the satisfaction of achieving your goals (Nanette likes spreadsheets. She loves breaking down goals into all the moving parts to see how to accomplish the final result. Jules cringes at the word spreadsheets, and you say that word too often, she has nightmares about being trapped in the "cells."), but it is important to be careful when setting goals as well. If you do not meet a goal or two (or ten), do not beat yourself up. No one ever achieves every goal they ever set; if they do, their goals aren't challenging them enough. Goals are meant to help you grow and evolve into a better you, and growing pains are part of this process.

As with everything else in your writing career, take the time to review and assess your goal-setting and goal-achieving processes. Are you setting goals that are too lofty? Are you setting goals that aren't pushing you enough? Do you have a good variety of short- and long-term goals so that you can measure your progress on any given day? Have you set up a reward system?

Ah, yes, the reward system. This is one of the best parts about setting goals. When you are defining your goals, make sure you identify one level where you will be rewarded for succeeding, as this will further solidify the satisfaction you experience and make you want to replicate it. For example, let's say that your goal is two write one thousand words on your current project every day for two months. When you achieve your goal for seven days straight, you might reward yourself with a box of Godiva chocolates. When you achieve it every day for the first month, you treat yourself to a movie. When you achieve the full goal, writing every day for two solid months, you book yourself a one-hour massage.

It is important that the rewards be appropriate for the achievements. For example, if you reward yourself with the massage after seven days and the box of chocolates after two months, you might feel a sense of disappointment with the chocolate reward because it doesn't live up to the massage reward (of course, some of you will argue this point, which is why you need to define rewards that work for you).

Rewards may not work for everyone. They don't work for Nanette because when she wants the reward, she just goes out and gets it, whether she has achieved the goal or not. For her, the sense of accomplishment is stronger and more gratifying than any tangible reward, and that's okay. Part of the journey of building a healthy writing career is discovering what works for you and recognizing that what works for others may have less or no effect on you.

External Fanning of the Flames

External efforts to stoke your dragon's fire focus on eliminating distractions, practicing self-care, and building a supportive community.

Eliminate Distractions

A productive environment is defined differently for everyone. Some people need music playing or other background noise when they write; others need absolute silence. Some people do better by writing early in the morning, whereas others prefer afternoons or late at night. Some people can put words on the paper whenever they have a few minutes to spare; others need blocks of time to write. Some writers enjoy the feel of a pen in their hand while others prefer the clacking of the keyboard under their fingers. You and you alone can define what a productive environment is for you, and that definition can change based on what project you are working on and even where you are in the project (just starting out, deep in the thick of it, or tying up any loose ends).

If you have been incorporating the journaling activity into your writing process, you have hopefully been able to identify some factors that work well for your writing as well as some that need to be avoided. When you consider your writing set-up, it is important to think about all aspects of the environment. Are you sitting, standing, or reclining? Are you connected to the internet? Do you have a beverage or snack nearby, if you need them? Do you have sufficient lighting? Is the temperature comfortable for you? What about your mental state: Are you focused on the here and now? Obviously we should do our best to eliminate any distractions that we identify, but we should also make an effort to include what helps us succeed.

To identify possible distractions, consider all of your senses. What makes your eyes the most comfortable when working? Nanette uses a dark screen on her computer to minimize eye strain. Julia needs bright light, preferably in the form of sunshine streaming through windows. What causes your eyes to drift away from the task at hand? Nanette is more productive when she is in a room with windows that have limited views (if she can see too much through the windows, she gets distracted, as does her dog, who then has to interrupt her all the time to tell her about everything he is seeing). What about your ears—what makes them most comfortable and what interferes with your writing focus? Do you prefer to have music playing? White noise, like muted conversations or the television in the background? Or absolute silence? Think about your hands, arms, shoulders, and posture: What is comfortable for you? What is not? Do you need certain tastes at the ready or does having food and drink at hand offer you an opportunity to procrastinate? What about smells? Nanette does really well with earthy smells, but perfumes will send her to the pharmacist or ER (allergy issues), so she has to be very careful about any smells that might invade her writing space.

In addition to the five senses, think about ambient issues, such as temperatures. Nanette cannot write (or do much of anything, really) if the back of her neck is cold (which honestly earns her some strange looks when she's writing in a coffee shop during a triple-digit summer heat wave and has a scarf wrapped around her neck). Another often overlooked area is emotional or mental distractions. If you're worried about paying an upcoming bill or concerned about a sick friend, it can be harder to focus on your writing.

This might be a good time to meditate so you can let go of the emotional work for now in order to get your writing done. If you know that a certain activity might spark a reaction that will hinder your writing, don't engage in that activity before your writing sessions. For example, Jules has a strong reaction to certain people in an online writing group. The group gives her great insights, but certain people's comments can be quite frustrating. (Nanette here: They're ridiculously frustrating.) Recognizing that she might react to these interactions, Jules doesn't access those communities until after she has met her writing goals for the day.

Scheduling online activity for later in the day is a great way to minimize distractions, especially if you are prone to get lost on social media for hours or are one of those people with forty-seven tabs open on your web browser at all times (Nanette raises her hand in shame). If you find avoiding the online social worlds difficult, look into productivity extensions for your web browser (e.g., WasteNoTime). These extensions can be used to limit the time spent on specific websites to certain periods of time during the day or for a total number of minutes. When you reach that limit, the website is blocked for a defined period of time. Sure, there are always ways to get around these blocks, but sometimes just getting that warning that your online activity will be blocked is enough to make you realize you've spent far too long surfing the internet and need to get back to writing.

Practice Self-Care

Self-care is critical to a healthy writing career. We really can't stress that enough. It is especially important for ensuring that your dragon remains fierce and focused because, without you, your dragon doesn't exist. Taking the necessary steps to ensure that you get adequate sleep, nutrition, and physical activity can increase your production during your writing sessions.

When we think about the fires burning inside us, motivating us to write, we might get the idea that we have to get all the words out on the paper now, before we lose them and they're gone! But building a healthy writing career requires a long-term perspective. The words will be there when you are ready to write them. We need to make sure that you are in a position to write them when you need them.

Sometimes when we are having a difficult time calling forth our dragons and their fire, it might help to step away from the writing. Yes, that sounds counterintuitive, but taking a break can help you reignite your passion and your drive to succeed. When we take a break, it doesn't mean running off to Tahiti and lying on the beach, doing nothing but soaking up the sun (you can do that once you have achieved your vision of success). It also doesn't mean forgetting about or ignoring the writing and just assuming it will return to us when we return to our writing environment. Taking a break means shifting gears, whether in the way you think, move, or look at the world around you. You are actually still engaged in your writing process, but you are approaching it in a new way.

When you take a break, you should physically move away from your writing area. Stand up and move your body in new ways (different from when you are writing). Go for a walk. Wash the dishes. Dance around your living room. Stand in the sunshine and breathe deeply, shaking out any kinks in your neck, back, and wrists. Spend a few minutes staring at a point on the horizon. If you work on screens for much of the day, it is important to stretch your eyes as one of your muscle groups. Staring at different points along the horizon can help minimize the eyestrain that you experience (whether you realize it or not) when working on a computer screen. It is also good to look at different colors than what you normally see on your screens, so go outside and look at some trees or the sky or even your neighbor's funky red door (but don't be a peeping Tom, please).

This is also a good time to practice meditation, especially if you are feeling distracted or blocked while writing. In addition, you can review your visualization process if you are feeling less than motivated. Revisit your vision of success, focusing on how good it will feel when you get there. As you move back to your writing, take a moment to visualize yourself achieving that success through your writing. Vocalize it with an optimistic goal as you sit down to write once more.

If you worry that taking a break during your writing session will "interrupt your flow," then before you step away from your writing, make a note of what you will write next (i.e., as soon as you return from your break). You can also write the first part of a sentence, leaving it unfinished. When you return from your break, read the unfinished sentence and your brain will pick up right where you left off, especially as it is feeling refreshed and has more revitalizing blood flowing through it.

You should also build longer breaks into your writing schedule/plan. Planning a few days away from your writing can help you avoid burnout while replenishing your creative reserves, especially if you do another creative activity during that time away, such as attending a concert, making a cake, or going dancing. Jules takes the weekends off from writing, which helps her refill her creative reserves and keeps her dragon's fire burning brightly throughout the week. Use your planned breaks well, and they will keep moving you closer to your vision of success.

. . .

Build a Supportive Community

The final external area of focus is finding a community that supports you in your writing process. Communities can be tricky environments. You want to find people who are just slightly ahead of you in their writing careers so they inspire you to achieve a goal that is within your reach. If they are too far ahead or focused on something that doesn't mesh well with your vision of success, you will end up feeling frustrated or even resentful.

Your community should have similar goals as you do. For example, don't join a group that focuses on writing one book a month if your realistic plan is to write a book every six months. Of course, communities are often bigger than a single focus, so it is important that you recognize what information and insights you want to glean from the community and which ideas you want to let go of or ignore. You should always be open to learning something new, because you never know when that information might benefit your writing process and move you closer to achieving your vision of success. But don't get so distracted by Shiny Object Syndrome that you careen down a rabbit hole that doesn't connect to your vision of success. Periodically reviewing your goals and visions can help get you back on track if you get distracted by a new technological development, service, or idea. It can also help you identify when you need to revise your goals and vision to incorporate a new development that will get you to your vision of success in a more streamlined manner.

Finally, don't be afraid to walk away from any community if it becomes toxic to your personal approach to your writing career. Remember, your dragon is uniquely your own. Others' dragons will not benefit you. If someone in a community tries to convince you otherwise, determining that their approach or their process is the only way to succeed, that community may not be the right one for you.

Action Step #4

Building on the work you did in Action Step #3, define a series of short- and long-term goals for achieving your vision of success. Develop goals for one week, one month, six months, one year, three years, and five years. Make sure each of your goals is a SMART goal.

If you want to, share you goals in the Healthy Writing Career Facebook group to get feedback and see how other people are setting goals to achieve success.

5-DON'T LET THE FIRE CONSUME YOU

Sephora is giving us a knowing look. We've come to that point in the book where we have to offer a word of caution.

Dragons are powerful beings, and when they agree to share their power with us, we can become mesmerized by the fire that burns within us. Power is good. Fire is good. Both drive you toward your vision of success in a meaningful and productive way.

However, as with all good things, too much of it can warp your sense of reality and become destructive. Respect the power of the dragon. Use it, but don't abuse it.

Just like with any power, you can become addicted, and an addiction to writing is just as unhealthy as an addiction to alcohol or drugs. Someone who becomes addicted to writing may start to ignore others and even ignore their own self-care because they are too focused on getting all the words written. They may become so lost in the world they are creating in their writing that they don't leave the house, cancel meet-ups with friends, and forget to go grocery shopping so they rely on fast food and energy drinks for all their meals (if they remember to eat). This is not healthy behavior for anyone, and it's one of the reasons that we repeatedly stress the need to take scheduled breaks and step away from the writing process.

The truth is that the writing process is more than just putting words on the page. You also have to experience the world outside your own limited environment. Whether you are writing historical novels, action adventure screenplays, free verse poems, news articles, self-help books, short stories, or blog posts, you have to go out into the world and see what is happening so that you can effectively translate the ideas in your head into words that the world outside will understand and relate to.

If you give in to the power of the fire and let it consume you, you will never reach your vision of success, even if you think you are working toward it because the addiction will force you to forsake everything for it. Shutting yourself off from your friends, family, and community is ultimately doing a disservice to your writing, and as you take more and more of the fire from your dragon, it will shrivel up to a shadow of its fiercest self. Even if you can endure and avoid burnout long enough to get your project done, it will no longer be writing that is inspired or that creates meaningful connections to your readers. It will feel lifeless, and you will feel defeated. After all, you gave up everything to get this project completed and now no one can appreciate it!

You gave up everything. That's a key warning sign right there.

Writing should be an enjoyable process for you, and the outcome should create an enjoyable experience for your readers. Yes, you might have to sacrifice some of your time and energy to achieve your vision of success, but your dragon should never require extravagant costs or excessive losses. (No one's dragons should demand virgins for sacrifice!) Writing should add to your life, not take away from it. When you develop a healthy writing career, it is a career that is balanced, allowing time for your writing process as well as time to find inspiration, connect with readers, spend time with friends and family, and generally live a fulfilling life.

Action Step #5

Set up a schedule to review and revise, as necessary, your vision for success and specific goals for achieving your vision. Incorporate regular breaks into your schedule, including times to hang out with friends and family, activities to replenish your creative well, and events that let you engage in your community. By adding these items to your schedule, you are reaffirming that being part of the world around you is an important component of your successful writing career.

6-LETTING YOUR DRAGON FLY FAST AND CONFIDENTLY

Sephora is outside now, doing some warm-up stretches as she gets ready to welcome a whole slew of new dragons. She is excited to teach them how to soar through the skies, flying confidently toward your visions of success.

Building a healthy and successful writing career doesn't happen by chance, and if you are struggling to stay motivated and moving forward, you might need to spend some time creating and nurturing your dragon. Such efforts are well spent as they will enable you to harness the power and determination to succeed at achieving whatever life you want to create for yourself.

Remember, you are in control of your writing career, including what you produce and how you produce it. No, you cannot control how others react to what you create, but when you put in the work and stay true to yourself and your goals, your creative endeavors will attract people who want to support you.

Don't be distracted by all the shiny objects that are erupting on the writing scene. If you find something that you feel might benefit your writing career, evaluate it based on the vision of success that you have defined. Does the new toy really deliver what you need? Does it fit within your process in a way that will benefit you? Or is it something that creates more work for you and takes you away from the writing process?

When you have a definitive vision of where you want to be, it makes all the little decisions along your path easier to work through because you can focus on two key points: does it move you closer to your vision of success or does it offer new insights that make you want to adjust your vision of success? If the answer is no to both questions, move along, knowing that you do not need to interrupt your writing process. Indeed, you are on a journey of building the writing career of your dreams.

Go forth and fly fast and confidently!

ABOUT THE AUTHORS

Nanette M. Day

Dog wrangler, cat slave, turkey observer, cow racer, raccoon enabler...these are just a few of the jobs that keep Nanette busy on her acreage. When she's not watching Mother Nature's songbirds, quadrupeds, and creepy crawlies, Nanette writes books detailing their shenanigans. In addition to writing humorous vignettes of how her dog and cats are taking over the world (one nap at a time), she writes gritty flash fiction and short stories as well as small-town romance novels.

You can find Nanette at www.NanetteMDay.com

J.S. Dixon

Fuzzy sock collector, martini connoisseur, and dandelion enthusiast, author Jules Dixon writes contemporary M/F and LGBT romance, including the Triple R Series of seven New Adult romance titles, the M/M cowboy contemporary romance series Cherry County Cowboys, including *Spurs, Chaps,* and *Whips.* She also writes the popular multi-story series Holiday Hotties of short MM holiday-inspired stories as Rowan Nash. And now the Building a Healthy Writing Career and Productive Author non-fiction series. She loves tackling hard subjects with a little humor and a spark of sizzle.

You can find Jules at:

www.julesdixon.com

http://www.facebook.com/JulesDixonAuthor

https://twitter.com/JulesofTripleR

https://www.pinterest.com/JDixonAuthor

https://www.instagram.com/julesdixonauthor/
https://bookandmainbites.com/JulesDixonAuthor

Nanette M. Day

Puppy Kisses Book 1

Mover and shaker. Squirrel chaser. Love muffin. Blanket hog.

For a dog in the country, it's important to run faster than the bunnies through the acreage obstacle course, greeting the turkeys and deer as they enjoy the breakfast buffet, chasing down any pesky raccoons who think they own the place, checking on the opossums to make sure they're not just "playing dead" (fool me once...), and serenading the neighborhood cows—all while keeping an eye on all those squirrels and their shenanigans.

Puppy Kisses is full of (mostly truthful) stories about the escapades of Pistachio, a dog on a mission to be everybody's friend (except maybe those pesky raccoons).

C. Jai Ferry

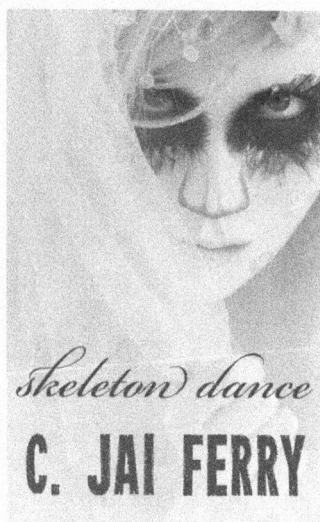

Skeleton Dance

"My grandmother wanted to kill me..."

So begins a dark and disturbing look into a world that is all too real for thousands of children every day. "Skeleton

Dance" is the story of one young girl's perseverance in surviving the eccentricities of her grandmother. Despite being harassed in a multitude of ways, this young girl is able to stand up to her grandmother in both small and grandiose ways. Sometimes victorious, but more often not, she ultimately grows into a woman faced with the biggest challenge yet: Follow the well-worn path of the matriarchs in her family or strike out into virgin territory.

2014 winner of the Vermillion Literary Project Short Story Contest.

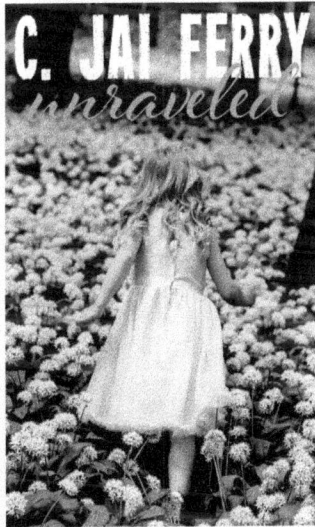

Unraveled: A collection of flash fiction and short stories

Step into a world of struggling fathers, aging English teachers, terrified mothers, plague-bearers, revenge artists, ill-fated lovers, and children searching for their place in life —all characters brought to life in the flash fiction of C. Jai Ferry. Ferry uses evocative language and imagery to highlight those telling moments when a person's entire life changes from a seemingly simple decision. These bite-sized morsels, most fewer than 100 words, examine the human condition and all its bittersweet moments.

J.S. Dixon

Essential Secrets for Building Successful Writing and
Critique Groups: Productive Author Series

https://www.amazon.com/J-S-Dixon/e/B07YGSTRBJ/

https://www.amazon.com/Jules-Dixon/e/B00PUSNF90/

https://www.amazon.com/Rowan-Nash/e/B07YF448MC/

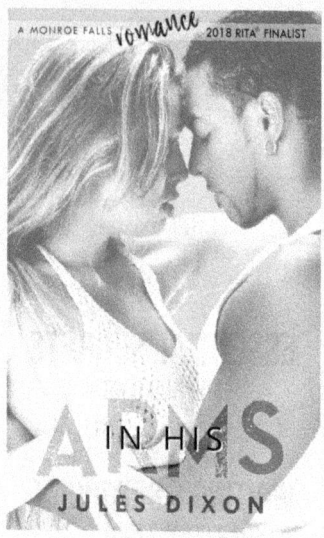

2018 RITA Finalist

In His Arms: A Monroe Falls Romance

Ten years ago Kiera Redfern left Monroe Falls and moved father and farther away. An invitation to the opening of a time capsule triggers the vague memory of her contribution and prompts her return. No one needs to see that letter, and definitely not Zach Lorton. When heated memories become fresh temptation, Kiera has to decide between changing the past or fighting for her future.

Zach never thought she'd be there, but after a night of revelations and a kiss that can't be ignored, he's ready to help Kiera heal from the past. When his boss demands his return to NYC, Zach has a choice to make—continue the abuse that's followed him through his childhood or stand up for himself and be the man he wants to be for Kiera.

Both will find out... is it better to be forgiven or forgotten?

In His Arms was originally part of the *Falling: Small Town Love Anthology.*

Triple R Series (A rainbow of love!)

Run to Love: Triple R 1

Personal trainer Jude Saylor's sense of direction in life has always been a little questionable. After a move and new job, he seems to be on the right path—until a cautious and sweet new client enters into the picture. Soon Jude wonders if happiness isn't as simple as a direction, but if it could be the woman he has next to him on the journey.

Presley Bradenhurst is a go-getter, as evidenced by her hundred pound weight loss, but the alteration to the outside didn't quite transfer to the inside. When Presley's trainer is fired and Jude steps up as the one who wants to make her sweat, will her instinct to run keep her from knowing a love she's only dreamed about?

In the end, can a lost soul and a broken soul work it out?

Rest, My Love: Triple R 2

~Editor's Pick~

Ex-soldier Rahl Vendetti returned to his hometown after watching three of his friends die. He should've died too. The guilt weighs on him and every breath is fed by a demon of war that taunts his future.

Singer and interior designer Sage Whiteman hit a genetic jackpot when it comes to dying young. She's living on borrowed time, so letting people in isn't easy, but the bartender with teddy bear eyes makes her wonder if it's time to open up.

They have plenty of chemistry between the sheets, but do they have the ability to be what the other needs outside of the bedroom, too? Sage may be the angel to bring out the gentle giant in Rahl, but can he be the strength she needs to face her uncertain future? Will they save each other and create something unexpected?

Ride With Love: Triple R 3

Motorcycle shop manager Kanyon Hills prides himself on being an honest and upstanding guy until a past one-night stand walks into his life and lets him know that he helped create the bubbling five-year-old, Grace.

Soon he's given a choice—his child or his girlfriend, Willow. His choice haunts him every day. Chef Willow Harper puts everyone's needs and happiness before her own. When Kanyon announces they are over, he creates a deep fissure in her heart, but her sixth sense tells her that a love like theirs will never truly be over and her heart will wait.

Can Willow learn to put herself first and find her own happiness with or without Kanyon? Will Kanyon grow from his past mistakes and return to the woman who fills his heart's crevices, or will he sacrifice his heart to the woman who had his child?

Road to Love: Triple R 4

Playboy Oliver Aston never hid who he is from anyone, and he finds it hard to understand when someone does just that. Betrothed at birth to the local town sweetheart, cowboy Holt Jamison spent his life believing that revealing his true self would disappoint his family, but after finding his heart's other half, that justification is getting harder and harder to stand by.

After a heated lovers quarrel in the desert, Oliver is sent back to the States alone and wondering if he's not one who's meant for love. When Holt leaves the military and moves far from his Alabama home to Oliver's hometown, is it a second chance the two hearts deserve? Or will a woman from the past come knocking to stake a claim on one of them?

Ready for Love: Triple R 5

Advertising account executive Jace Zelensky has a lover that won't ever have a heart beat.

Personal trainer and former soldier Kai Thomas worries that when it comes to love her heart may have been permanently broken at a young age.

When Jace's blind commitment to her job interferes with Kai's attempts to make a true connection and leaves Kai searching for her neurotic dog, Waffles, can Jace come to the rescue? Will a night with a no-strings-attached promise be the release they both need to satisfy their curiosity, or will those few minutes lead to something they're willing to risk their hearts for?

Ribbons of Love: Triple R 6

Avery Knicely grew up with three older brothers who can't see her as anything but the family's baby. What she really wants and needs is twisted with doubts, but after the ways of her brothers, she's positive she doesn't need a man to hover over her.

Security specialist Bryson Welch's controlling and manipulative twin sister reminds him on a daily basis why he joined the army and why he never should have returned home to endure the toxic relationships his sister and mother perpetuate. A blind date leads to a cold but eye-opening night in his vehicle and fulfills a Christmas wish for Bryson.

Will he be able to show Avery he can take care of her in the ways she really needs without overpowering her? Or will family come between the young lovers and lead Avery to question his true intentions?

Rescued by Love: Triple R 7

Aurora Jessen lives a life that would make a princess envious, but will her prince ever find her with her overprotective father hovering? When the infuriating Drexel Mason returns to town, his ability to get her to almost spontaneously orgasm while simultaneously making her want to stab him fascinates her, but a deadly accident reiterates the lack of control over her own life.

Drexel Mason's childhood was more a scene from a nightmare than a tale of fated love. The memories make him cover his pain with a secret elixir, but Aurora's kiss confiscates the lingering ache. When she accidentally takes his pain-killing potion, he's given an opportunity to slay the dragon of his cruel past and release the prince hiding inside.

Will Drexel save his princess or will she continue waiting for true love in her ivory tower?

Cherry County Cowboys Series

Spurs: Cherry County Cowboys 1

M/M Romance

Dr. Grayson Taylor is convinced that a summer fling with the bartending cowboy is a quick remedy to mend his broken heart. Soon his plans to return to big city lights for a dream career don't seem as attractive as the cowboy with dimples lying in his bed. When Grayson's charred past reappears, can he learn that forgiveness costs less than pride and admit he is the one who needs to be healed?

Cowboy Izaac Scott drove into town with little more than boots on his feet, a well-loved baseball cap on his head and a cross-country journey on his mind, but he's not sightseeing. He's running from the ghost of a first love. Will the doctor be the one to help Izaac realize that true love can heal the past or will the cruel spurs of life jab him in the heart again?

Chaps: Cherry County Cowboys 2

M/M romance

Rising rodeo star Nate O'Neill never expected to be living in a small Nebraska ranching town waiting for his rodeo brother to recover from a vicious ride. His unplanned stop steers him into the arms and bed of local celebrity, Tennessee Reed. Soon he questions what thrills him more —the rodeo or Tenn. Forced to face his reckless past, he's reminded that relationships can cause damage far worse than any bull ride ... and maybe he's headed for the same suffering again.

Professional football draft-pick Tennessee Reed returns home emotionally shattered by the unexpected passing of his father who left Tenn with a hereditary secret buried in his chest. He might be dying inside, but when Nate walks into his life all Tenn's troubles seem to disappear into those hazel eyes and he's never felt more alive. Will Tenn follow the cowboy wherever life leads? Or will he protect his heart and watch those fringed leather chaps ride away?

Whips: Cherry County Cowboys 3

Dune Wexley's unrelenting efforts to take down a local crook ended his law enforcement career and his father's life. Dune's lived in seclusion ever since. A Sunday drive to check on his mysteriously disappearing herd of cattle ends with a guest in his house, one who makes him reconsider isolating his shielded heart. But can this stranger be trusted?

Mason LaFleur answered an ad in the paper that held the promise of becoming a real cowboy on an authentic ranch, but that never happened. Instead Mason was forced to run away from a cruel man, but a miscalculation finds him bouncing off the hood of a truck and into the arms of a genuine cowboy.

When Mason is kidnapped, Dune must decide if getting revenge for his father's death is more important than saving the man who's offered up his heart and life to heal the broken cowboy.

Owned by the Alpha: Manlove Edition

M/M Romance

"Owned by the Alpha: manlove Edition is highly recommended!" —TBR Pile Reviews

NEW Dark Paranormal Romance Stories by International Bestselling Evernight Authors!

The Alpha lives for the hunt...

Driven by instinct, an Alpha shifter recognizes his fated mate from one scent, one touch. He'll pursue his man, regardless of the cost, and anyone else would be smart to get out of his way. He won't stop until he takes possession of his prize.

Although the hunter doesn't need convincing, his mate certainly does. The Alpha will have to prove himself as a lover and convince his man that he plays for keeps.

Includes stories: A Tiger's Luck by Maia Dylan, Last Alpha Standing by James Cox, **Mooncrest by Jules Dixon,** His Guardian Panther by Elena Kincaid, The Scarf by L.J. Longo, A Matter of Trust by Pelaam, Conflict of Interest by L.D. Blakeley

Checkered Flag Series

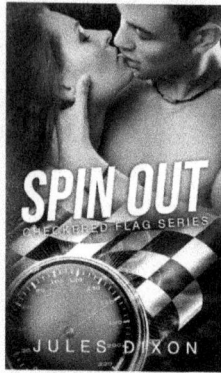

SPIN OUT: Checkered Flag Series 1

Reagan Breckle lost two things after leaving Linden
College... eighty pounds and her crush on racing prodigy
Thayr Westfield. Her passion for racing has brought her to
the ISCaR Formula 1 racing competition where she has the
chance to prove herself and beat Thayr at his own game.
Even though she tries to fight them, the intense feelings she
had for Thayr return. When her team's car is sabotaged and
their sponsoring professor goes missing, Reagan's
leadership is tested and her dream is jeopardized. How can
she protect her heart, when she needs Thayr to save her
dream?

Thayr Westfield is shocked he never noticed Reagan when
she was on his team, but he's definitely noticing her now.
His heart burns for her, but he questions if she'll let him in
when he broke her trust a year ago? When his estranged

birth father shows to the competition, and a dream internship goes awry, Reagan is the only part of his life that feels right. But when Reagan needs him, will Thayr be able to get past the deep hurt he suffered as a child and ask the one person who was never there for him to help the woman he loves?

Coming Soon!

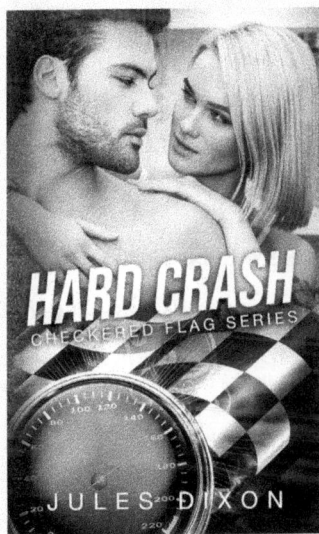

HARD CRASH: Checkered Flag Series 2

The story of Max Bowen and Savannah Monroe. They say rubbin' is racin' and these two put that saying to the test.

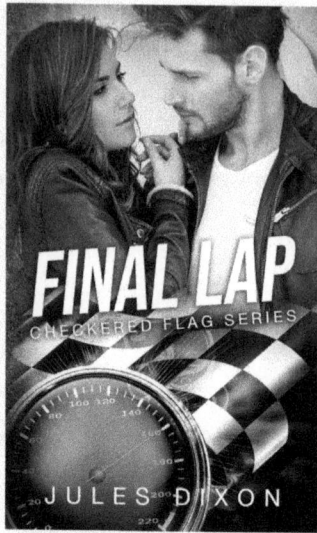

FINAL LAP: Checkered Flag Series 3

The story of Cameron Jones and Sophie Oestmann Find out what happens when two lovers race to the finish line.

Holiday Hotties by Rowan Nash

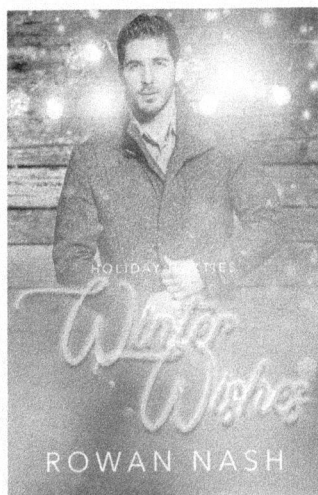

Winter Wishes

A sexy Santa, a matchmaking Aunt, and a wish he never thought would come true.

Sexy Santa was never on his list, but Caleb Gilden stopped writing a Christmas wish list long ago. Santa had always come up short in fulfilling his wishes. That's why he's put all of his money and time into his gift shop—at least others can get what's on their wish list.

Reeve Stone wishes for a different outcome of a day when his parents died in a horrific car crash right in front of him and his sister. He knows that isn't going to happen, so he'll just keep a smile on his face for his sister's sake.

But when Reeve meets the green-eyed gift shop owner and is forced into donning a Santa suit for a sick and disadvantaged children's holiday party, will he finally grant a wish for Caleb?

And will Caleb help Reeve through the hardest day of the year only to discover love is what they've both been wishing for?

Snowflake Smiles

A blizzard, a moody Christmas tree farmer, and a chance to be what each other needs.

Race car driver Ben Carver's trip home takes a detour when the storm of the decade dumps on his plans. With no available hotels, he's committed to riding out the storm and holiday in a restaurant until his phone buzzes and a stranger announces he's come to save Ben from a Christmas alone. Ben's ready for a new challenge in his fast-moving life, but the brooding tree farmer might have too many secrets that will keep them from getting their relationship to the checkered flag.

Christmas tree farmer Ford Lennox returned to western Nebraska after his parents passed away in quick succession and left unanswered questions about how he really came into the world. He dedicates himself to reviving his parent's business and giving holiday happiness to others, much to the detriment of his personal life, but one night snowed in with the comfort of the blazing fire and a man who makes his heart race might change his thinking. He's hidden too much for too long and maybe the past doesn't matter as much as the future does.

Will Ford end up being the best Christmas gift Ben's ever received? Find out now!

Frozen Faith

A dream on the line, a hockey date that's not to watch the game, and a man whose heart has been frozen by past relationships.

Dayne Swift didn't imagine the last-hope loan for his business would be accompanied with a flirty loan officer, but he'll take both. After coming out, Dayne's family told him don't come back and since then, he's kept to himself, only confiding in one other person—his ex-girlfriend from college—and she's cheering him onto the goal.

Burned one too many times by love, Will Howard knew the opportunity to invest in Dayne's business was the right call, and Will can't help but think the sweet and nervous furniture designer is worth taking a chance on, too. He asks Dayne to join him at a hockey game, but little does Dayne know he'll be on the ice and not in the stands.

When the loan's in jeopardy, can Dayne come up with a different plan for his business to save his future and can Will find the faith to believe Dayne is worth fighting for when he's frozen with memories of past choices?

Champagne Cheers

A failing business, a man with the means to save it, but in the end, they might find they both need to be saved.

Aspiring venture capitalist Matteo Bianci III has one chance to prove himself to his brutally honest father or his dreams of becoming a partner in the Bianci business will be over.

Sent to asses the return potential of several Niagra-on-theFalls area vineyards, Matteo's short business visit turns into an unplanned vacation when a lake-effect blizzard causes whiteout conditions and the airport closes. Matteo's attraction to the bed and breakfast and vineyard's owner isn't in his future plan, the solid plan he's had since his was fourteen. Falling can't happen, but still he wonders, what it would be like to have someone to kiss on New Year's Eve.

Janek Becker's vineyard is struggling, so when the stubborn rich guy shows at his door declaring he has a reservation in his closed bed and breakfast, Janek's torn between turning him away into the snow or making a pitch to the man who could save his future. When the vineyard's generator stops working and equipment breaks in the fermenting house threatening the year's wine, can they work together to save the crop?

Will Matteo realize a good endeavor when he sees one and invest his heart? Or will he decide that the Three Cheers Winery and Janek aren't worth the risk?

Other stories to come:

ROWAN NASH

Puppy Presents

Two adorable puppies, two men with broken hearts, and the chance for all to have a happy new year.

This year Kiel Rushton wishes for something with a beating

heart and maybe a wagging tail. A trip to the local shelter finds him facing a tough decision when he discovers that two dogs, Mistletoe and Holly, are destined not to see the New Year. He's never had a fish, much less a dog. The kennel worker with twinkling eyes seems to think he could handle the responsibility, but responsibility has always been Kiel's middle name.

Brady Littleton works the shelter every Saturday, more reliable than even the postal delivery person. When it comes to a dog being the right fit for someone, his gut has never been wrong, but it's been wrong about a man being his right fit—way too many times. The timid soon-to-be dog owner just needs some encouragement and maybe a doggie play date with his own dog to show him the season is meant for caring.

Will Brady be able to convince Kiel the two dogs were meant to be in his life? Will Kiel convince Brady that he was meant to be there, too?

Jingle Bell Joy

Candy Cane Cupid